NAME

COPYRIGHT

All rights reserved. No part of this planner may be reproduced in any form without expressed permission from the publisher, except in the case of brief quotations.

This planner should not be considered a legally binding document. It is recommended you consult with a lawyer to create a formal, legally binding will regarding your desired final wishes and arrangements should you become incapacitated, or upon passing.

The author, publisher, and all those involved in the creation of this workbook, under any and all circumstances, are not considered responsible or liable for any damages that come from its content or purchase. Use of this planner is meant entirely for the benefit of the purchaser in the organization and documentation for end of life wishes and preferences.

It is a good idea to ensure those involved in your end of life planning and arrangements are notified of this document and its location. Important, sensitive and private content such as personal identification information and passwords are included in the following pages, and it is essential this information not become misplaced to avoid the risk of identity theft or misuse of any kind.

The owner and users of this document takes full responsibility for the safekeeping, accuracy, and content upon use. The user agrees this planner is considered an organizational workbook only, in which to record final wishes and desires relevant in the case of incapacitation or upon passing.

© 2020, Christian Scripture Journals and Planners

TABLE OF CONTENTS

Introduction
A Comprehensive, Easy to Customize, All-in-One Peace of Mind Planner

Personal Information
Name, Address, Family, Pets, and Dependents

At the Time of Passing
Who to Call, Contact List, and Special Instructions

Funeral Arrangements
Funeral and Burial Details, Special Requests, and Key Contacts List

Assets Overview
What My Loved Ones Can Expect; Assets Summary, Legal Documentation, Instructions, and Follow-Up Information

Christian Living
Church, Charities, Tithing, and Other Related Topics

Business Information
Business / Employment Details, Banking, Key Associates Contact List, and Follow-Up Instructions

Banking Information
Personal Banking / Accounts, Mortgage, Credit Cards, Legal, Contact List, and Follow-Up Instructions

Important Documentation
Personal ID, Will, Insurance, Executor, Power of Attorney, Medical / DNR, Legal, and Documentation Location

Insurance Essentials
Medical / Dental / Vision, Motor Vehicle, Life, Home Owner, Rental, Pet, and Insurance Information

Medical Information and Instructions
Power of Attorney Information, Conditions, Medication, DNR / Organ Donor, and if Incapacitated Instructions

Dependents and Guardianship
Names, Guardianship, Legal and Health Documents, Instructions of Care Instructions

Loose Ends to Tie Up
Cancel, Close, Pay, Change of Name and Follow-Up Instructions

Final Wishes and Instructions
Blank Notes Space for Important Instructions, Final Wishes, and Overflow Content

A Personal Message For My Loved Ones
Blank Notes Pages for Final Farewell Messages to Loved Ones

Signed and Dated
Last words

INTRODUCTION

Welcome to your Peace of Mind and Heart Christian Family Planner.

This book is designed to make life-planning as simple, user friendly, and stress-free as possible, and includes wonderful inspirational biblical quotes throughout.

Your Planner is a comprehensive, customizable, all-in-one workbook to record your vital information, personal wishes, and final messages to loved ones.

It is a valuable gift for those left behind so that they can ensure your instructions are fulfilled accordingly, and to help avoid duress or confusion by planning in advance.

We have provided plenty of space to customize each section as per your needs, and include additional overflow space at the end of the book if required. It is wise to begin with the initial personal identification section first, and then proceed to one chapter at a time, collecting all the documentation and information in advance for efficiency sake.

Remember to update this planner as changes to your circumstances arise, such as new employment, investments, insurance, or adjustments to your personal wishes.

Please remember, this planner is not considered a legal document and should not be considered a formal will.

<u>*Always store this workbook somewhere safe, to prevent sensitive, private information from getting into the wrong hands.</u>

"For I know the Plans I have for you," declares the Lord,
"Plans to Prosper you and not to harm you,
plans to give you Hope and a Future."

Jerimiah 29:11

PERSONAL INFORMATION

My Legal Name

_____
_____

Address

_____
_____
_____

Mailbox or P.O. Box Number

_____
_____

Mailbox Location

_____
_____

Key Location

_____
_____

Primary Phone Numbers

_____
_____

Family Members

Spouse's Name / Maiden Name
_____
_____

Children's Names
_____
_____
_____
_____
_____
_____
_____

Grandchildren's Names
_____
_____
_____
_____
_____
_____
_____

Dependents Overview List

My Dependents Names Include

Pets Names

Notes

Family Members and Dependents

Siblings Names

_____
_____
_____
_____
_____
_____

Mother's Name / Maiden Name

_____
_____

Father's Name

_____
_____

Ex-Spouse's Name/s

_____
_____
_____

Notes

_____
_____
_____
_____

"*Let us hold unswervingly to the hope we press, for He who promised is faithful.*"

Hebrews 10:23

AT THE TIME OF MY PASSING

Please Contact the Following People Immediately Upon My Passing or Incapacity

Spouse / Partner

Name

Contact Information

Notes

Healthcare Power of Attorney Agent

Name

Contact Information

Notes

Executor of Will

Name

Contact Information

Notes

Please Contact the Following Church Associates

Pastor

Church Name _____

Contact Information _____

Notes _____

_____

_____

Pastor #2

Church Name _____

Contact Information _____

Notes _____

_____

_____

Church Associate #1

Name _____

Contact Information _____

Notes _____

_____

_____

Church Associate #2

Name _____

Contact Information _____

Notes _____

_____

_____

Please Contact the Following Family, Friends, Church Members, and Associates

Name _____

Contact Information _____

Relationship _____

Name _____

Contact Information _____

Relationship _____

Name _____

Contact Information _____

Relationship _____

Name _____

Contact Information _____

Relationship _____

Name _____

Contact Information _____

Relationship _____

Name _____

Contact Information _____

Relationship _____

Name _____

Contact Information _____

Relationship _____

Please Contact the Following Family, Friends, Church Members, and Associates

Name

Contact Information

Relationship

Name

Contact Information

Relationship

Name

Contact Information

Relationship

Name

Contact Information

Relationship

Name

Contact Information

Relationship

Name

Contact Information

Relationship

Name

Contact Information

Relationship

Please Contact the Following Family, Friends, Church Members, and Associates

Name

Contact Information

Relationship

Name

Contact Information

Relationship

Name

Contact Information

Relationship

Name

Contact Information

Relationship

Name

Contact Information

Relationship

Name

Contact Information

Relationship

Name

Contact Information

Relationship

Please Contact the Following Family, Friends, Church Members, and Associates

Name

Contact Information

Relationship

Name

Contact Information

Relationship

Name

Contact Information

Relationship

Name

Contact Information

Relationship

Name

Contact Information

Relationship

Name

Contact Information

Relationship

Name

Contact Information

Relationship

Additional Key Contact Information

Accountant and Book Keeper

Name #1

Contact Information

Name #2

Contact Information

Notes

Lawyer #1

Name

Contact Information

Notes

Lawyer #2

Name

Contact Information

Notes

Estate Planner

Name

Contact Information

Notes

Additional Key Contact Information

Financial Planner

Company and Agent Name _____

Contact Information _____

Financial Planner

Company and Agent Name _____

Contact Information _____

Stock Broker

Company and Agent Name _____

Contact Information _____

Business Employer / Associate

Company and Agent Name _____

Contact Information _____

Business Employer / Associate

Company and Agent Name _____

Contact Information _____

Business Employer / Associate

Company and Agent Name _____

Contact Information _____

Additional Key Contact Information

Health Care Provider – Medical

Company and Agent Name

Contact Information

Health Care Provider – Dental

Company and Agent Name

Contact Information

Health Care Provider – Vision

Company and Agent Name

Contact Information

Health Care Provider – Other

Company and Agent Name

Contact Information

Veterinarian

Company and Agent Name

Contact Information

Veterinarian

Company and Agent Name

Contact Information

Contact Information – Notes

"Trust in the Lord forever, for the Lord,
the Lord himself, is the rock eternal."

Isaiah 26:4

FUNERAL ARRANGEMENTS

Funeral Arrangements Contact Person

Location

Contact Information

Church

Name of Primary Priest

Contact Information

Funeral Home

Address

Contact Information

Cemetery or Crematorium

Plot / Address

Contact Information

Funeral Insurance Policy

Company Name

Contact Information

Notes

Funeral Arrangements

Burial

Headstone Details

Cremation

Ashes to be shared with / spread at

Obituary

Please Include the Following

Funeral Arrangements - Celebration of Life Services

Please Read the Following Farewell to My Loved Ones During Service (Christian Values, Lessons, Encouragement, Etc.)

Funeral Arrangements – Notes

"Come to me, all of you who are weary
and carry heavy burdens,
and I will give you rest."

Matthew 11:28

ASSETS OVERVIEW – WHAT MY LOVED ONES CAN EXPECT

Personal Residence Address

Note: Please see will for detailed instructions and division of assets

_____
_____
_____

PO Box Location and Address

_____
_____

Partner / Co-Owner Names

_____
_____

Contact Information

_____
_____

Legal Will Location and Instructions for Division of Assets

_____
_____
_____
_____
_____
_____

Assets Overview

Keys Location and Miscellaneous Instructions

_____
_____
_____

Alarm and Security Information

_____
_____
_____

Utilities Warranties and Documentation Location

_____
_____
_____

Upkeep Information and Document Location (Gardener, Etc.)

_____
_____
_____

Notes

_____
_____
_____
_____
_____
_____
_____

Assets Overview

Real Estate Investment - Second Property Address

_____

_____

Type of Property (Residential / Commercial)

_____

_____

PO Box Location and Address

_____

_____

Partner / Co-Owner Names

_____

_____

Contact Information

_____

_____

Legal Documentation Location and Instructions

_____

_____

Assets Overview

Keys Location and Miscellaneous Instructions

_____

_____

_____

Alarm and Security Information

_____

_____

_____

Utilities Warranties and Documentation Location

_____

_____

_____

Upkeep Information and Document Location (Gardener, Etc.)

_____

_____

_____

Notes

_____

_____

_____

_____

_____

_____

_____

Assets Overview

Vehicle List: Car, Motorcycle, Recreation Vehicle, Snowmobile, Etc.

Vehicle

Year/Make/Model

VIN – ID

Ownership Documentation Location

Lease / Load Information

Keys Location

Notes

Vehicle

Year/Make/Model

VIN – ID

Ownership Documentation Location

Lease / Load Information

Keys Location

Notes

Assets Overview

Vehicle List:

Vehicle _____

Year/Make/Model _____
_____

VIN – ID _____

Ownership Documentation Location _____

Lease / Load Information _____

Keys Location _____

Notes _____
_____
_____
_____
_____

Vehicle _____

Year/Make/Model _____
_____

VIN – ID _____

Ownership Documentation Location _____

Lease / Load Information _____

Keys Location _____

Notes _____
_____
_____
_____
_____

Assets Overview

Vehicle List:

Vehicle _____

Year/Make/Model _____

_____

VIN – ID _____

Ownership Documentation Location _____

Lease / Load Information _____

Keys Location _____

Notes _____

_____

_____

_____

_____

Vehicle _____

Year/Make/Model _____

_____

VIN – ID _____

Ownership Documentation Location _____

Lease / Load Information _____

Keys Location _____

Notes _____

_____

_____

_____

_____

Assets Overview

Investments: Stocks, Mutual Funds, and Other

Type

Location

Account Number

Contact Person

Documentation Location

Notes

Type

Location

Account Number

Contact Person

Documentation Location

Notes

Type

Location

Account Number

Contact Person

Documentation Location

Notes

Assets Overview

Investments:

Type

Location

Account Number

Contact Person

Documentation Location

Notes

Type

Location

Account Number

Contact Person

Documentation Location

Notes

Type

Location

Account Number

Contact Person

Documentation Location

Notes

Assets Overview

Investments:

Type

Location

Account Number

Contact Person

Documentation Location

Notes

Type

Location

Account Number

Contact Person

Documentation Location

Notes

Type

Location

Account Number

Contact Person

Documentation Location

Notes

Assets Overview

Insurance Benefits:

Policy Type _____

Location _____

Account Number _____

Contact Person _____

Documentation Location _____

Notes _____
_____
_____
_____

Policy Type _____

Location _____

Account Number _____

Contact Person _____

Documentation Location _____

Notes _____
_____
_____
_____

Policy Type _____

Location _____

Account Number _____

Contact Person _____

Documentation Location _____

Notes _____
_____
_____
_____

Assets Overview

Employer Benefits #1

Name

Account Number

Contact Person

Documentation Location

Notes

Employer Benefits #2

Name

Account Number

Contact Person

Documentation Location

Notes

Employer Benefits #3

Name

Account Number

Contact Person

Documentation Location

Notes

Assets Overview

Retirement Benefits

Name

Account Number

Contact Person

Documentation Location

Notes

Retirement Benefits #2

Name

Account Number

Contact Person

Documentation Location

Notes

Social Security

Name

Account Number

Contact Person

Documentation Location

Notes

Assets Overview

Other: Veteran's Benefits, Etc.

Name

Account Number

Contact Person

Documentation Location

Notes

Other:

Name

Account Number

Contact Person

Documentation Location

Notes

Other:

Name

Account Number

Contact Person

Documentation Location

Notes

Assets Overview

Money Owed to Me

Name

Account Number

Contact Person

Documentation Location

Notes

Name

Account Number

Contact Person

Documentation Location

Notes

Name

Account Number

Contact Person

Documentation Location

Notes

Assets Overview

Personal Items, Jewelry, and Heirlooms

Item

Location

Notes

Item

Location

Notes

Item

Location

Notes

Item

Location

Notes

Assets Overview

Personal Items, Jewelry, and Heirlooms

Item

Location

Notes

Item

Location

Notes

Item

Location

Notes

Item

Location

Notes

Assets Overview

Personal Items, Jewelry, and Heirlooms

Item

Location

Notes

Item

Location

Notes

Item

Location

Notes

Item

Location

Notes

Assets Overview

Personal Items, Jewelry, and Heirlooms

Item

Location

Notes

Item

Location

Notes

Item

Location

Notes

Item

Location

Notes

Assets Overview

Storage Company #1

Name

Address

Key Location or Combination Number

Storage Company #2

Name

Address

Key Location or Combination Number

Notes and Instructions

Honour the LORD with thy substance,
and with the first-fruits of all thine increase:
So shall thy barns be filled with plenty,
and thy presses shall burst out with new wine.

Proverbs 3:9-10

CHRISTIAN LIVING

Church, Charities, Tithing, and Other Related Topics

The following include my personal requests and instructions regarding Church, Tithing, Charity Donations, Etc.

Church

Church

Church, Charities, Tithing, and Other Related Topics

Charities

Charities

Church, Charities, Tithing, and Other Related Topics

Tithing

Tithing

Church, Charities, Tithing, and Other Related Topics

Other Related Topics

Other Related Topics

"For if we live, we live to the Lord,
and if we die, we die to the Lord.
So then, whether we live or whether we die,
we are the Lord's."

Romans 14:8

BUSINESS INFORMATION

Business Details

Business Name _____

Business Type _____

Address _____

_____

Landlord Name _____

Contact Information _____

Lease Documentation Location _____

Partner / Co-Owner Name _____

Contact Information _____

Partner / Co-Owner Name _____

Contact Information _____

Partner / Co-Owner Name _____

Contact Information _____

Partner / Co-Owner Name _____

Contact Information _____

Keys Location _____

Notes _____

_____

_____

Business Information

Associates, Employees, and Contractors

Name

Contact Information

Name

Contact Information

Name

Contact Information

Name

Contact Information

Name

Contact Information

Name

Contact Information

Name

Contact Information

Name

Contact Information

Notes

Business Information

Name

Contact Information

Name

Contact Information

Name

Contact Information

Name

Contact Information

Name

Contact Information

Name

Contact Information

Name

Contact Information

Name

Contact Information

Notes

Business Information

Bank Name

Address

Contact Information

Business Bank Account Number

Business Bank Account Number

Credit Card Number

Username / PIN

Credit Card Number

Username / PIN

Documentation Location

Notes

Bank Name

Address

Contact Information

Business Bank Account Number

Business Bank Account Number

Credit Card Number

Username / PIN

Credit Card Number

Username / PIN

Documentation Location

Notes

Business Information

Accountant Name

Contact Information

Lawyer

Contact Information

Insurance Agency / Agent

Contact Information

Notes on Income, Royalties, Key Accounts Etc.

Online Business Information

Business Website Name

Hosting Provider

Username and Password

Website Developer Name

Contact Information

Documentation Location

Online Income Stream #1

Online Income Stream #2

Partner / Co-Owner Name

Contact Information

Partner / Co-Owner Name

Contact Information

Partner / Co-Owner Name

Contact Information

Business Email Address Name

Username and Password

Business Email Address Name

Username and Password

Business Email Address Name

Username and Password

Notes

Notes: Instructions for Domain Name Renewal, Hosting, Expenses, Etc.

Online Business Information

Online Business Information

Social Media

Name

Username and Password

Name

Username and Password

Name

Username and Password

Name

Username and Password

Name

Username and Password

Name

Username and Password

Name

Username and Password

Name

Username and Password

Name

Username and Password

Online Business Information

Accounts

Name

Username and Password

Name

Username and Password

Name

Username and Password

Name

Username and Password

Name

Username and Password

Name

Username and Password

Name

Username and Password

Name

Username and Password

Name

Username and Password

Online Business Information

Accounts

Name

Username and Password

Name

Username and Password

Name

Username and Password

Name

Username and Password

Name

Username and Password

Name

Username and Password

Name

Username and Password

Name

Username and Password

Name

Username and Password

Name

Username and Password

Business Information

Money I Owe to Others

Person / Company Name

Contact Information

Documentation Location

Notes

Person / Company Name

Contact Information

Documentation Location

Notes

Person / Company Name

Contact Information

Documentation Location

Notes

Person / Company Name

Contact Information

Documentation Location

Notes

Additional Notes

Business Information

Additional Notes and Instructions

"For the Spirit God gave us does not make us timid,
but gives us power, love and self-discipline."

2 Timothy 1:7

BANKING INFORMATION

Note: Please secure this document due to its sensitive information, (ideally in a safe), or place specific sensitive information somewhere separate with instructions to access as desired.

Bank Name

Account Type and Number

Account Type and Number

Bank Online Web Address

Username and Password

Debit Card Number

Credit Card Number

CV and Password

Online Username and Password

Rewards

Notes

Bank Name

Account Type and Number

Account Type and Number

Bank Online Web Address

Username and Password

Debit Card Number

Credit Card Number

CV and Password

Online Username and Password

Rewards

Notes

Banking Information

Bank Name

Account Type and Number

Account Type and Number

Bank Online Web Address

Username and Password

Debit Card Number

Credit Card Number

CV and Password

Online Username and Password

Rewards

Notes

Safe Deposit Box

Bank Location

Box Number

Key Location

Contents

Safe Deposit Box

Bank Location

Box Number

Key Location

Contents

Banking Information

Other Credit: Credit Cards, Line of Credit, Department Stores, Etc.

Name

Account Number

Online Website

Username and Password

Name

Account Number

Online Website

Username and Password

Name

Account Number

Online Website

Username and Password

Name

Account Number

Online Website

Username and Password

Name

Account Number

Online Website

Username and Password

Notes

Banking Information

Other Credit: Credit Cards, Line of Credit, Department Stores, Etc.

Name

Account Number

Online Website

Username and Password

Name

Account Number

Online Website

Username and Password

Name

Account Number

Online Website

Username and Password

Name

Account Number

Online Website

Username and Password

Name

Account Number

Online Website

Username and Password

Notes

Banking Information

Other Credit: Credit Cards, Line of Credit, Department Stores, Etc.

Name

Account Number

Online Website

Username and Password

Name

Account Number

Online Website

Username and Password

Name

Account Number

Online Website

Username and Password

Name

Account Number

Online Website

Username and Password

Name

Account Number

Online Website

Username and Password

Notes

Banking Information

Mortgage, Line of Credit, Loans

Mortgage Details

Bank / Lender

Contact Information

Account Number

Documentation Location

Second Mortgage Details

Bank / Lender

Contact Information

Account Number

Documentation Location

Third Mortgage Details

Bank / Lender

Contact Information

Account Number

Documentation Location

Other

Bank / Lender

Contact Information

Account Number

Documentation Location

Notes

Banking Information

Line of Credit

Bank / Lender

Contact Information

Account Number

Documentation Location

Line of Credit

Bank / Lender

Contact Information

Account Number

Documentation Location

Other

Bank / Lender

Contact Information

Account Number

Documentation Location

Other

Bank / Lender

Contact Information

Account Number

Documentation Location

Notes

Banking Information

Loans: Cars, Student Loan, Etc.

Bank / Lender _____

Contact Information _____

Account Number _____

Documentation Location _____

Bank / Lender _____

Contact Information _____

Account Number _____

Documentation Location _____

Bank / Lender _____

Contact Information _____

Account Number _____

Documentation Location _____

Bank / Lender _____

Contact Information _____

Account Number _____

Documentation Location _____

Bank / Lender _____

Contact Information _____

Account Number _____

Documentation Location _____

Notes _____

_____

_____

"For God so loved the world, that he gave his only Son,
that whoever believes in him should not perish
but have eternal life."

John 3:16

IMPORTANT DOCUMENTATION LOCATION

Will

_____

_____

Notes _____

_____

Health Care Power of Attorney Papers

_____

_____

Notes _____

_____

Passport

_____

_____

Notes _____

_____

Birth Certificate

_____

_____

Notes _____

_____

Important Documents Location

Social Security Card

Notes

Drivers Licence

Notes

Marriage Certificate

Notes

Tax Documents

Notes

Divorce Papers

Notes

Important Documents Location

Life Insurance

Notes

Health Insurance - Medical

Notes

Health Insurance Location – Dental

Notes

Health Insurance Location - Vision

Notes

Health Insurance Location – Other

Notes

Important Documents

Funeral Insurance

Notes

Vehicle Insurance #1

Notes

Vehicle Insurance #2

Notes

Vehicle Insurance #3

Notes

Home Owner Insurance

Notes

Important Documents Location

Rental Home Insurance

_____

_____

Notes _____

_____

Children's Insurance #1

_____

_____

Notes _____

_____

Children's Insurance #2

_____

_____

Notes _____

_____

Children's Insurance #3

_____

_____

Notes _____

_____

Other Family / Dependents Insurance

_____

_____

Notes _____

_____

Important Documents Location

Pet Insurance #1

Notes

Pet Insurance #2

Notes

Storage Insurance #1

Notes

Storage Insurance #2

Notes

Additional Notes

Important Documents Location

Other

_____

_____

Notes

Other

_____

_____

Notes

Other

_____

_____

Notes

Other

_____

_____

Notes

Other

_____

_____

Notes

Other

_____

_____

Notes

Important Documents Location - Notes

Jesus said to her, "I am the resurrection and the life.
Whoever believes in me, though he die, yet shall he live,
and everyone who lives and believes in me shall never die.
Do you believe this?"

John 11: 25 - 26

INSURANCE PROVIDER INFORMATION

Health Insurance – Primary Health

Company Name _____

Agents Name _____

Contact Information _____

HSA (Health Savings Account) Information _____

_____

Health Insurance - Dental

Company Name _____

Agents Name _____

Contact Information _____

Notes _____

Health Insurance – Vision

Company Name _____

Agents Name _____

Contact Information _____

Notes _____

Health Insurance – Medical

Company Name _____

Agents Name _____

Contact Information _____

Notes _____

Additional Notes _____

_____

Insurance Information

Life Insurance #1

Company Name

Agents Name

Contact Information

Notes

Life Insurance #2

Company Name

Agents Name

Contact Information

Notes

Vehicle Insurance #1

Company Name

Agents Name

Contact Information

Notes

Vehicle Insurance #2

Company Name

Agents Name

Contact Information

Notes

Vehicle Insurance #3

Company Name

Agents Name

Notes

Insurance Information

Home Owner Insurance

Company Name

Agents Name

Contact Information

Notes

Rental Home Insurance

Company Name

Agents Name

Contact Information

Notes

Children's Insurance #1

Company Name

Agents Name

Contact Information

Notes

Children's Insurance #2

Company Name

Agents Name

Contact Information

Notes

Children's Insurance #3

Company Name

Agents Name

Contact Information

Notes

Insurance Information

Other Dependents Insurance

Company Name

Agents Name

Contact Information

Notes

Pet Insurance #1

Company Name

Vets Name

Contact Information

Notes

Pet Insurance #2

Company Name

Vets Name

Contact Information

Notes

Storage Insurance #1

Company Name

Agents Name

Contact Information

Notes

Storage Insurance #2

Company Name

Agents Name

Contact Information

Notes

Insurance Information

Funeral Insurance

Company Name

Agents Name

Contact Information

Notes

Other Insurance

Company Name

Agents Name

Contact Information

Notes

Other Insurance

Company Name

Agents Name

Contact Information

Notes

Other Insurance

Company Name

Agents Name

Contact Information

Notes

Other Insurance

Company Name

Agents Name

Contact Information

Notes

Insurance Information - Notes

"For since we believe that Jesus died and rose again, even so, through Jesus, God will bring with him those who have fallen asleep."

1 Thessalonians 4:14

MEDICAL INFORMATION

Health Care Power of Attorney

Name _____

Contact Information _____

Notes _____

Do Not Resuscitate Instructions Document Location

_____

_____

Notes _____

_____

_____

Organ Donor Instructions Document Location

_____

_____

Notes _____

_____

_____

Blood Type

_____

_____

Primary Care Physician

Name _____

Contact Information _____

Address _____

Notes _____

Medical Information

Medical Conditions

Medications

Medical Information

Allergies, Food Sensitivity, and Reactions

If Incapacitated Please Follow Below Requests (Further Details in DNR Document)

Medical Information

Preferred Hospital

Name

Contact Information

Address

Notes

Pharmacy

Name

Contact Information

Address

Notes

Caregiver Company / Person #1

Name

Contact Information

Address

Notes

Caregiver Company / Person #2

Name

Contact Information

Address

Notes

Medical Information - Notes

But they who wait for the Lord shall renew their strength;
they shall mount up with wings like eagles;
they shall run and not be weary;
they shall walk and not faint.

Isaiah 40:31

DEPENDENTS INSTRUCTIONS OF CARE

My Dependents

Name

Relationship

Contact Information

Personal Documentation Location

Health Conditions Documentation Location

Guardianship Instructions Documentation Location

Guardian Name

Contact Information

Primary Care Physician

Contact Information

Notes

My Dependents

Name

Relationship

Contact Information

Personal Documentation Location

Health Conditions Documentation Location

Guardianship Instructions Documentation Location

Guardian Name

Contact Information

Primary Care Physician

Contact Information

Notes

My Dependents

Name _____

Relationship _____

Contact Information _____

Personal Documentation Location _____
_____

Health Conditions Documentation Location _____
_____
_____
_____

Guardianship Instructions Documentation Location _____
_____

Guardian Name _____

Contact Information _____
_____
_____
_____

Primary Care Physician _____

Contact Information _____

Notes _____
_____
_____
_____

My Dependents

Name

Relationship

Contact Information

Personal Documentation Location

Health Conditions Documentation Location

Guardianship Instructions Documentation Location

Guardian Name

Contact Information

Primary Care Physician

Contact Information

Notes

My Dependents

Name

Relationship

Contact Information

Personal Documentation Location

Health Conditions Documentation Location

Guardianship Instructions Documentation Location

Guardian Name

Contact Information

Primary Care Physician

Contact Information

Notes

My Dependents

Name

Relationship

Contact Information

Personal Documentation Location

Health Conditions Documentation Location

Guardianship Instructions Documentation Location

Guardian Name

Contact Information

Primary Care Physician

Contact Information

Notes

My Dependents – Pets

Name / Type of Pet _____

Name of Veterinarian _____

Contact Information _____

Address _____

_____

License, Insurance, and Documentation Location _____

_____

Health Conditions _____

_____

_____

Medications _____

_____

_____

Guardianship Instructions Documentation Location _____

_____

Guardian Name _____

Contact Information _____

General Instructions of Care – Food, Habits, Exercise, Sleep, and Other Needs

_____

_____

_____

_____

_____

My Dependents – Pets

Name / Type of Pet _____

Name of Veterinarian _____

Contact Information _____

Address _____

_____

License, Insurance, and Documentation Location _____

_____

Health Conditions _____

_____

_____

Medications _____

_____

_____

Guardianship Instructions Documentation Location _____

_____

Guardian Name _____

Contact Information _____

General Instructions of Care – Food, Habits, Exercise, Sleep, and Other Needs

_____

_____

_____

_____

_____

My Dependents – Pets

Name / Type of Pet _____

Name of Veterinarian _____

Contact Information _____

Address _____

_____

License, Insurance, and Documentation Location _____

_____

Health Conditions _____

_____

_____

Medications _____

_____

_____

Guardianship Instructions Documentation Location _____

_____

Guardian Name _____

Contact Information _____

General Instructions of Care – Food, Habits, Exercise, Sleep, and Other Needs

_____

_____

_____

_____

_____

My Dependents – Notes

"May the God of hope fill you with all joy and peace as you trust in him, so that you may overflow with hope by the power of the Holy Spirit."

Romans 15:13

LOOSE ENDS TO TIE UP

Follow Up: Cancel, Close, Pay, Change of Name, Etc.

Example: Hydro, Electric, Phone, Cable, Internet, Storage, Credit Cards, Autopay, Banking...

Company _____

Contact Information _____

Account Number _____

Username and Password _____

Notes _____

Company _____

Contact Information _____

Account Number _____

Username and Password _____

Notes _____

Company _____

Contact Information _____

Account Number _____

Username and Password _____

Notes _____

Company _____

Contact Information _____

Account Number _____

Username and Password _____

Notes _____

Loose Ends to Tie Up

Company

Contact Information

Account Number

Username and Password

Notes

Company

Contact Information

Account Number

Username and Password

Notes

Company

Contact Information

Account Number

Username and Password

Notes

Company

Contact Information

Account Number

Username and Password

Notes

Loose Ends to Tie Up

Company _____

Contact Information _____

Account Number _____

Username and Password _____

Notes _____

_____

Company _____

Contact Information _____

Account Number _____

Username and Password _____

Notes _____

_____

Company _____

Contact Information _____

Account Number _____

Username and Password _____

Notes _____

_____

Company _____

Contact Information _____

Account Number _____

Username and Password _____

Notes _____

_____

Loose Ends to Tie Up

Company _____

Contact Information _____

Account Number _____

Username and Password _____

Notes _____

_____

Company _____

Contact Information _____

Account Number _____

Username and Password _____

Notes _____

_____

Company _____

Contact Information _____

Account Number _____

Username and Password _____

Notes _____

_____

Company _____

Contact Information _____

Account Number _____

Username and Password _____

Notes _____

_____

Loose Ends to Tie Up Online:

Email, Website, Hosting, Social Media, Banking, Amazon eBay, Memberships

Company _____

Contact Information _____

Account Number _____

Username and Password _____

Notes _____

_____

Company _____

Contact Information _____

Account Number _____

Username and Password _____

Notes _____

_____

Company _____

Contact Information _____

Account Number _____

Username and Password _____

Notes _____

_____

Company _____

Contact Information _____

Account Number _____

Username and Password _____

Notes _____

_____

Loose Ends to Tie Up Online:

Company _____

Contact Information _____

Account Number _____

Username and Password _____

Notes _____

_____

Company _____

Contact Information _____

Account Number _____

Username and Password _____

Notes _____

_____

Company _____

Contact Information _____

Account Number _____

Username and Password _____

Notes _____

_____

Company _____

Contact Information _____

Account Number _____

Username and Password _____

Notes _____

_____

Loose Ends to Tie Up Online:

Company _____

Contact Information _____

Account Number _____

Username and Password _____

Notes _____

_____

Company _____

Contact Information _____

Account Number _____

Username and Password _____

Notes _____

_____

Company _____

Contact Information _____

Account Number _____

Username and Password _____

Notes _____

_____

Company _____

Contact Information _____

Account Number _____

Username and Password _____

Notes _____

_____

Loose Ends to Tie Up Online:

Company _____

Contact Information _____

Account Number _____

Username and Password _____

Notes _____

_____

Company _____

Contact Information _____

Account Number _____

Username and Password _____

Notes _____

_____

Company _____

Contact Information _____

Account Number _____

Username and Password _____

Notes _____

_____

Company _____

Contact Information _____

Account Number _____

Username and Password _____

Notes _____

_____

"For I consider that the sufferings of this present time
are not worth comparing with the glory that is to be revealed to us."

Romans 8:18

FINAL WISHES AND INSTRUCTIONS

Final Wishes and Instructions

Final Wishes and Instructions

Final Wishes and Instructions

"The LORD himself goes before you and will be with you;
he will never leave you nor forsake you.
Do not be afraid; do not be discouraged."

Deuteronomy 31:8

MESSAGES FOR MY LOVED ONES

A Personal Message for:

A Personal Message for:

A Personal Message for:

A Personal Message for:

A Personal Message for:

A Personal Message for:

NOTES

Notes

Notes

Notes

For none of us lives to himself, and none of us dies to himself.
For if we live, we live to the Lord, and if we die, we die to the Lord.
So then, whether we live or whether we die, we are the Lord's.
For to this end Christ died and lived again, that he might be
Lord both of the dead and of the living.

Romans 14:7-9

LAST WORDS

_____
_____
_____
_____
_____
_____
_____
_____
_____
_____

Signature

_____

Name and Date

_____

Printed in the USA
CPSIA information can be obtained
at www.ICGtesting.com
LVHW080203270923
759476LV00019B/300